iOS 17
—— User Guide ——

iOS 17

— User Guide —

THE COMPLETE GUIDE TO THE LATEST VERSION OF APPLE'S MOBILE OPERATING SYSTEM

DAVID WEST

CONTENTS

INTRODUCTION

The next significant update to Apple's iOS mobile operating system for the iPhone and iPod Touch is called iOS 17. It was revealed on June 5, 2023, during the company's Worldwide Developers Conference (WWDC), and a September 2023 release is anticipated.

The features of iOS 16 are improved and expanded upon in iOS 17, which brings many fresh features. Improvements to the Home Screen, Lock Screen, and Safari are among these, in addition to new features for Messages, FaceTime, and Photos.

Whoever wants to understand more about iOS 17 should read this book. This user guide will provide you with the knowledge you need, whether you are an experienced user looking to learn about the newest features or a novice iPhone user.

CHAPTER 1

GETTING STARTED WITH THE iOS 17

You must update your iPhone to the newest software version to use iOS 17. Also, it would be best if you had an iPhone 8 or later to update to iOS 17. Additionally, you can update your iPod touch (7th generation), iPad Pro (all models), iPad (5th generation and after), and iPad mini (5th generation and later).

Alternatively, go to Settings > General > About to see if your Apple device is compatible. Your device's model number can be found under "Model." You can then compare your device's model number with the ones mentioned above to see if it is compatible with iOS 17.

If compatible, go to Settings > General > Software update to begin the update process. You will see a button to download and install iOS 17 if available.

Before you upgrade the software on your iPhone, make a backup. If something goes wrong during the upgrade process, this will assist you in protecting your data.

When updating your iPhone, be patient. It may take time to update. Once the update has been applied to your iPhone, explore the brand-new options. Take the necessary time to become familiar with everything because there is much to learn.

You can also update your device via iTunes on a computer as a second option. Compared to updating wirelessly on your smartphone, updating via iTunes on a computer gives you more control over the update procedure.

What You'll Need Is:

➤ Your computer's most recent installation of iTunes

➤ An iOS 17-compatible iPhone or iPad

➤ A Lightning cable for your computer and gadget

➤ Adequate battery life on your gadget

► A device with enough capacity on it to accommodate the iOS update file

It's critical to backup your smartphone before updating in case something goes wrong when installing the update. To do this:

► Utilize a Lightning cable to connect your iPhone or iPad to your computer.

► On your PC, launch iTunes. ITunes will recognize your linked gadget.

► In iTunes, click the device icon in the upper-left corner.

► To choose where to save the backup, click "This Computer" in the Backups section.

When the backup is finished, click "Back Up Now" once more. Depending on how much data you have, this can take some time.

How to Download the iOS Update

After backing up your device, you can start downloading the most recent iOS update from Apple's servers:

Click the "Check for Updates" button in iTunes.

Once connected, iTunes will search Apple's servers for available iOS upgrades for your device.

If one is discovered, click the "Download" button next to the update listing. Avoid unplugging your device during the download because doing so can stop it.

The iOS update download will begin. Depending on your internet connection speed, the download could take a while because the file size usually is around 2GB.

You might need to attempt again until the complete iOS update file can be downloaded successfully if any error warnings appear during the download process.

How to Install iOS 17 Update

You may now use iTunes to install iOS 17 onto your device after downloading the software:

► Keep your gadget plugged into your computer. Verify that iTunes recognizes your device.

► In iTunes, click the symbol for the connected device.

► Click the "Check for Update" or "Update"

button while holding down the Option or Shift keys on a Mac or Windows computer. ITunes will then install the downloaded update file as a result.

➤ You will see a warning asking you to accept the terms before you can install iOS 17. Click "Agree."

➤ Your smartphone will now start receiving iOS 17 updates from iTunes. Don't unplug or mess with the connection while this is happening.

➤ A progress bar displaying the updated installation's current state will appear. The installation process can take up to an hour, so be patient.

➤ Your device will reboot after the update is finished, at which point you will be prompted to complete some initial setup steps. Obey the directions displayed on the screen.

➤ Your device will have iOS 17 loaded completely once the setup is complete! Now, you can take it out of your computer.

Important Advice

► Before updating, ensure iTunes and your computer are running the most recent versions.

► Instead of using a hub, attach your device directly to a USB port on your computer.

► Don't disconnect your device mid-update or stop the update installation.

► Several reboots may occur on your device while the update is being applied. That is typical.

► Restart the update procedure if you receive any error warnings or other problems.

► If something goes wrong, you can protect your data by backing up your device.

CHAPTER 2

NEW FEATURES/ IMPROVEMENTS OF THE iOS 17

The new features and improvements in iOS 17 will revolutionize how you use your iPhone. The following are the iOS 17's new features and improvements:

A new lock screen

The lock screen is the first thing you see when you turn it on, so it needs to be both informational and aesthetically pleasing. With iOS 17, you have more flexibility over the lock screen. Widgets for the weather, calendar, and news can now be added to the lock screen. Additionally, you can configure various lock screens for various activities or times of day.

Added Widget Positional Flexibility

Now, widgets can be positioned practically anywhere on the Home screen, including the empty areas at the top and bottom. More adaptable widget positioning enables more excellent layout optimization.

To relocate widgets:

► Long-tapping an app icon will activate jiggle mode.

► To move widgets above or below other programs, tap and drag them.

► For a fresh appearance, position them around the top or bottom edges.

Enhanced Widget Stacking

Widgets can be stacked one on top of the other. To create a stack, drag one widget on top of another. To access different widgets, swipe through the stack.

Stacking widgets:

➤ Long pressing an app will activate jiggle mode.

➤ Drag and drop one widget over the other.

➤ Thus, a widget stack will be produced. To access the widgets, swipe through the stack of cards.

Animated Widgets

Now that some widgets feature interactive controls, managing apps is possible from the Home screen.

Interactive widget usage:

➤ Add qualifying widgets, such as music, notes, or a calendar.

➤ They will show interactive controls when used.

➤ Instead of opening the whole app, tap or slide the controls on the screen.

Customizing the Background of a Widget

Each widget's backdrop, color scheme, and level of transparency can be changed to suit your preferences. Match them to your wall covering.

Widget background editing:

- ► On a widget, press the info icon to activate jiggle mode.
- ► Select Transparency or a Background Colour.
- ► To make the widget blend in better, choose a color and/or opacity.

Widgets for Live Activity

The new Live Activities widgets provide a quick peek at dynamically updating information from apps like sports scores, rideshare journeys, food delivery, and more.

Adding Live Activities:

- ► On the Home screen, hold down a long press.
- ► For the widget gallery to appear, tap the Add button.

- ➤ To add them, look for widgets marked "Live Activities."

- ➤ Real-time updates will be made to the data!

Third-party Widgets

In iOS 17, third-party apps can extend widget capabilities alongside Apple's widgets. Social media, chat, music, and utility widgets are to be expected.

Identifying fresh third-party widgets

- ➤ Long-pressing a blank spot on your Home screen will bring up the widget gallery.

- ➤ Look through the catalog for widgets marked with app names.

- ➤ To add a new widget to your home screen, tap + on it.

Homescreen Folders

On the Home screen, you can now make "Smart Folders" that automatically group apps based on categories like "Productivity," "Photos," "Social," etc.

Creating Smart Folders

- ► To access the menus when in jiggle mode, tap the + icon.
- ► Choose New Smart Folder, then choose a category.
- ► The Smart Folder will display apps that fit the category.

Custom Icons for First-Party Apps

Apple's standard system apps can now modify the icons on the Home screen. Adapt to your preferences!

To change the icons:

- ► To alter an icon, long-press it. Click the ‑ button.
- ► Choose a new icon design, color, or style from the available choices.
- ► Your Home screen will refresh with the new icon.

CHAPTER 3

NOTIFICATION

The handling and presentation of incoming notifications on iPhone and iPad have been significantly improved with iOS 17. The newest news and events can be kept up to speed with the help of notifications, but they can sometimes be invasive. Notifications are now less invasive and more informative in iOS 17. You can now snooze alerts or have them discreetly sent to avoid being interrupted.

Notification Summary

Enable Notification Summary to receive a daily digest of non-time-sensitive alerts at a specified time. This prioritizes less significant pings.

To use Notification Summary:

► Visit Settings and select Notifications.

► Turn on Scheduled Notifications under Scheduled Summary.

► To choose a delivery time or app, select Customise Summary.

Timing-Related Notifications

Time-sensitive warnings are prioritized by iOS and appear right away. Calls, messages, and real-time events are displayed as they occur.

Sensitive notification management:

▶ Turn on Time Sensitive in Settings > Notifications > Scheduled Summary.

▶ Only urgent alerts will take precedence over your Summary agenda.

Settings for Synchronised Notifications

Across all devices enrolled in your iCloud account, notification settings, including on/off toggles, alerts, and quiet hours, are kept in sync.

Syncing notification preferences:

▶ Use the same iCloud account to log in to all devices.

▶ On each device, change the notification settings as appropriate.

▶ They will sync with iPhones, iPads, Macs, and other compatible devices.

Focus Mode

Now, each app has its own Focus feature for filtering notifications. Choose precisely which applications can take over in different Focus modes.

Per-app Focus Mode configuration:

► Choose a Focus mode under Settings > Focus.

► Toggle app overrides by tapping the Apps list.

Linked Notifications

To reduce spam, alerts connected to an initial notification are now grouped. To expand a collection of alerts, tap "More."

To control Linked notifications:

► The "More" section will group notifications that are similar or come in succession.

► To view each notice, select "More."

► Swipe away the primary alert to instantly clear the entire bundle.

Silence Unknown Callers

The "Silence Unknown Callers" option can automatically block and forward calls from unauthorized numbers to voicemail. This lowers the chance of spam.

To enable this:

► Navigate to Settings > Phone.

► Activate the toggle "Silence Unknown Callers"

► Calls made without a known contact will be silenced

Notification History

The notification history log in iOS 17 allows you to catch up on missed alerts. You can access this from Settings > Notifications > History.

To see the history of notifications:

► Navigate to Settings > Notifications > History.

► You'll notice notifications that were recently delivered, but you missed

► To view any past notice, tap it.

CHAPTER 4

NEW MESSAGES FEATURES

Messages is one of the most used iPhone apps, and iOS 17 enhances it with various new features. Messages can now be edited and sent again, and animated stickers from Live Photos can be made.

Editing Sent Messages

Did you unintentionally send a text with a typo? The content of an iMessage can now be changed for up to two minutes after it has been sent.

To change a message that has already been sent:

- ► To edit a message bubble, tap and hold it.
- ► Tap Edit Message from the menu.

➤ The message will become editable. Change as you see fit.

➤ To validate the edit, tap the blue checkmark.

Unsend Message

By holding down the text bubble for a long time after sending a message, you can now unsend it for up to two minutes in addition to editing. Go to the menu and select Unsend Message.

To Unsend a message:

▶ Long press the message bubble you want to delete.

▶ Go to the menu and select Unsend Message.

▶ The conversation will end with the message gone.

Mark Conversation as Unread

Want a prompt to remember to respond to a thread of messages later? You can manually flag conversations as unread in iOS 17.

Add to the unread list:

▶ On the message thread, swipe left.

▶ Go to the menu and select Mark as Unread.

▶ A new unread dot will appear in the thread.

SharePlay from messages

You can now start a SharePlay session directly from a Messages discussion to synchronize watching movies, listening to music, and more with friends.

Using SharePlay

► Tap the person's name at the top when messaging them.

► In the menu, select SharePlay.

► Select media for your group to watch or listen to.

► SharePlay begins so that you can experience in sync!

Live Activities

Thanks to the new Live Activities feature, you can monitor real-time activities like sporting contests, rides, food deliveries, etc., right from discussion threads.

To try Live Activities:

► Click on a message's supported Live Activity link.

► The top of the thread will display the live stream.

► To close and stop watching the action, scroll up.

Message Reactions

Want to react to a message quickly? To select an emoji reaction, long press a text bubble that you've received and select Reaction from the menu.

Use Message Reactions as follows:

► Press a message bubble repeatedly.

► From the quick menu, select Reaction.

► Choose an emoji to represent your response.

In-Message polls

On iOS 17, you can now make polls inside conversations in Messages, eliminating third-party survey requirements. This is excellent for surveys and quick decisions.

To create in-app polls:

► Tap the More button while still in the Message thread.

► Enter your poll question and poll choices after tapping New Poll.

► To share a poll in a discussion, tap Send Poll.

Reverse Send Delay

You can choose from 10 seconds to 1 minute as the time limit after pressing send before you can "unsend" a message. This helps you to avoid sending terrible SMS.

To personalize:

► Select Settings > Messages.

► Select a time frame under "Message Undo Send."

► That much time will be available to undo a message with the shake gesture.

CHAPTER 5

FACETIME ENHANCEMENTS

iOS 17 makes FaceTime a fantastic tool for staying in touch with friends and family, even better. Several new capabilities have been added to FaceTime, including utilizing FaceTime on Apple TV and making and sharing links to FaceTime calls.

SharePlay in FaceTime

With the addition of SharePlay to FaceTime, you can watch movies, listen to music, and more while on a call with friends. Everyone stays in sync with shared playback.

Use SharePlay in FaceTime as follows:

▶ Make a FaceTime call to a friend.

▶ When the SharePlay icon displays, tap it.

▶ Pick a show or album for the group to watch or listen to.

▶ The Shared playback begins for both of you!

Portrait Mode

FaceTime now has a Portrait mode that allows you to creatively blur your background while using it to frame your face.

Activating Portrait mode:

➤ Call a friend on FaceTime.

➤ To switch to Portrait mode, tap the star icon.

➤ Now, your background will be fuzzy.

➤ To exit Portrait mode, tap once more.

FaceTime Links

To book a FaceTime call in advance, you can now create links and share them with the people you wish to join.

To create and share a FaceTime link:

➤ Open FaceTime and select Create Link from the top menu.

➤ You can choose a name, invite up to 100 people, and select share options.

➤ Select Create Link. Now you can distribute that Link!

Call scheduling

You can schedule a call with someone if they aren't immediately available for FaceTime.

To set up a FaceTime call for later:

- ▶ Start a new FaceTime call.
- ▶ Tap Schedule Call if they don't answer the phone.
- ▶ Decide on a time and day for the call.
- ▶ A calendar invite to join will be sent to them.

Live Captions

To make conversations more accessible, FaceTime can now automatically create live captions.

To activate Live Captions:

- ▶ Launch FaceTime and begin a new call.
- ▶ Choose Live Captions from the menu.
- ▶ The call's captions will now appear on the screen as you chat.

Hands off FaceTime

With the new Handoff capability, you can smoothly transfer FaceTime calls between your iPhone, iPad, and Mac.

To use Handsoff with FaceTime:

- ➤ On all compatible devices, sign in with the same iCloud account.
- ➤ On one device, begin a FaceTime call.
- ➤ To transfer the call to another device, launch FaceTime on that one.

Stage Light Effect

During FaceTime, the Stage Light effect adds classy studio lighting with a dark background to highlight your face.

Turning on the stage light

- ➤ Make a new FaceTime call.
- ➤ Select Stage Light by tapping the star icon.
- ➤ You suddenly have dramatic studio lighting shining on you!

CHAPTER 6

NEW PRIVACY FEATURES

Since privacy is crucial, iOS 17 comes with various additional features. Several new privacy features are included in iOS 17, including the option to block tracking URLs in Safari and to make it more challenging for apps to track your location.

App Privacy Report

The new App Privacy Report details how frequently apps access private information, including contacts, location, images, camera, and microphone. Track down problematic apps.

To view the report:

► Access App Privacy Report under Settings > Privacy & Security.

► Data access statistics for all apps will be displayed for the last seven days.

► To get detailed usage activity, tap any app.

Safety Check

You can instantly disengage from users and accounts using Safety Check and even withdraw app access as necessary. This is useful for relationships or compromises.

Safety Check usage:

► Activate Safety Check under Settings > Privacy & Security.

- ▶ Select the people, apps, and places you want to disconnect from by following the prompts.
- ▶ To carry out the data resets and access revocations, tap Continue.

iCloud Secure Keys

Store iCloud data with end-to-end encryption, including backups, notes, and photographs. The keys needed to decode the data are within your control.

To Activate Secure Keys:

- ▶ To access iCloud, go to Settings > [Your Name]> iCloud
- ▶ Select iCloud Secure Keys under Advanced Data Protection and set it on.
- ▶ Set a security key that is only accessible locally on the device.

Limited Photo Collection

Share a condensed, only-selected version of your iCloud Photos library with others. This keeps your photos private.

Using a limited library

- ► Open the Photos app, then add the allowed photos to a new album.
- ► In the album, click the Share button.
- ► Select Limited Library to create a link that only shares those specific images.

Local Processing of Live Captions

Now that Live Captions transcriptions are handled entirely on the device, discussions are kept more private. In eligible apps, tap the Live Captions button to enable.

How to utilize Live Captions

- ► Start a call using a compatible app like Face-Time.
- ► To enable transcriptions, tap the Live Captions icon.
- ► Your speech will only be locally transcribable on the device.

CHAPTER 7

NEW ACCESSIBILITY FEATURES

To make it easier for individuals with impairments to use their iPhones, iOS 17 comes with various new accessibility features. These include utilizing Voice-

Over to speak commands to your iPhone and Live Captions to view audio and video content captions.

Siri pause time

The time Siri pauses before responding to a spoken command automatically can now be adjusted. If you need more time to talk, lengthen the pause time.

Setting the Siri Pause Time:

▶ Use the slider to lengthen the pause before Siri responds by going to Settings > Accessibility > Siri.

▶ Siri will now wait for a more extended period after you finish speaking.

Live Captions

For the deaf and hard of hearing, iOS 17 adds system-wide Live Captions to instantly convert voice to text during calls, meetings, streaming media, and more.

How to utilize Live Captions

➤ Launch Control Centre and tap the Live Captions option to enable live captions.

➤ Live Captions will appear after you open a compatible app like FaceTime.

➤ To change the caption's font size, color, and other settings, tap the CC button.

Mirroring on the Apple Watch

The screen of your iPhone can now be wholly mirrored onto an Apple Watch. Excellent for magnified views or for wrist motions that initiate actions.

To enable screen mirroring:

➤ Link your iPhone and Apple Watch.

➤ Open Control Centre on your iPhone, then select Screen Mirroring.

➤ On the Apple Watch, select Enable. The entire iPhone screen is now mirrored on the watch!

The Background Sound

Ambient background sounds are now available on iOS 17 to cover annoying noises and foster a relaxing atmosphere. Excellent for improving sensory difficulties, tinnitus, or concentration.

Making use of Background sounds:

- ► Navigate to Accessibility > Audio/Visual > Background Sounds under Settings.
- ► Choose a calming backdrop, such as the sound of the ocean or a forest.
- ► To help you concentrate or unwind, play the sound. As necessary, adjust the volume.

Customized Apple Books fonts

You can now optimize custom fonts for reading difficulties like dyslexia in Apple Books. Additionally, font sizes are adjustable.

To change the fonts in Apple Books:

- ► To access Apple Books, go to Settings > Accessibility > Reading > Apple Books.
- ► Under Font Choices, choose the appropriate

fonts and text sizes.

► When you open a book in Apple Books, your preferred fonts will be used.

Buddy Controller

Buddy Controller allows friends to participate in a game by controlling specific elements. This is great for gamers with disabilities.

To make use of Buddy Controller:

► Connect your smartphone to two compatible wireless controllers.

► Start a game that is supported.

► Give a friend one of the controllers. They are now able to join in and participate in game control.

Standby Mode

A new function called StandBy mode enables your iPhone to enter a low-power state when unused. The battery life can be enhanced by doing this. Go to Settings > Battery > StandBy Mode to turn on StandBy mode.

Interactive Widget

Small applications known as widgets can be placed on the home screen or lock screen. Widgets are now interactive in iOS 17, allowing you to interact with them without opening the app. Long-press the home screen and then hit the + button to add an interactive widget.

Mood Tracking and Journalling

Mood Tracking is a brand-new feature in iOS 17. You can monitor your mood with this function throughout the day. Your submissions for mood can also have notes and tags added. Go to Settings > Health > Mindfulness > Mood Tracking to access the feature.

Shared AirTags and Airpod Improvements

To make it easier to locate things, you can attach AirTags, which are tiny tracking devices. AirTags can now be shared with others in iOS 17. The Batteries widget also displays your AirPods' battery level.

CHAPTER 8

SIRI

In iOS 17, Siri, Apple's voice assistant, gets a big makeover to improve its naturalness, responsiveness, and personalization. The most recent version includes upgrades for privacy, proactive recommendations, knowledge, speech recognition, and knowledge. Siri can now translate languages, respond to more complicated questions, and even operate smart home appliances.

Improved Voice Recognition

With iOS 17, Siri's speech recognition engine has been upgraded for greater accuracy. Users worldwide can now fully utilize voice commands thanks to Siri's improved ability to interpret various accents and dialects. Even in noisy situations, the assistant can hear and understand voices more clearly.

More prompt and contextual responses

Along with improving voice recognition, iOS 17 accelerates the rate at which Siri can analyze requests, provide pertinent information, or take action. With on-device processing, the assistant can now answer up to three times as quickly, and some requests can even be carried out without an internet connection. Siri's responses are also more contextual based on the user's usage history and personal information.

Additional Knowledge Base

The size of the knowledge graph that Siri uses for Q&A has doubled. The assistant can now intelligently respond to inquiries about various subjects, including sports scores, trivia about famous people, nutrition, and much more. As a result of the improved general knowledge, Siri can react to more general questions and follow-up inquiries.

Proactive suggestions

Siri will now provide proactive suggestions and shortcuts based on regular usage patterns and learned user behavior. For instance, suggesting a phone call to regular contacts during known times or bringing up upcoming meetings or events. Depending on the user's context, Siri may suggest using particular apps or settings.

Integration of Additional Apps

Siri is more tightly integrated with third-party apps in iOS 17. Users can now ask their favorite apps for information or access specific features using voice commands. Siri now has a considerably more comprehensive range of applications in the work, social networking, transit, retail, and other app areas.

Customized Using User Data

To provide personalized results, Siri may, with user permission, access pertinent personal information from apps such as Photos, Mail, Messages, and more. Instead of just conducting a generic online search, asking to "see photos from my trip" or "show me emails about work" results in exact, customized responses.

Language Support

In iOS 17, Siri adds the capacity to comprehend and transition between several languages with ease. Siri can now understand and converse in combinations like English and Spanish or Chinese and English for users who often speak multiple languages. The assistant recognizes the languages automatically.

Additional Privacy Protections

While iOS 17 gives Siri more data access, Apple has also strengthened privacy protections. Siri only uses information that is stored on the device. Users must consent to distribute audio recordings, and interactions must be anonymized. You can toggle access to apps on or off at any moment.

More options for natural voice

With more realistic voice options in iOS 17, Siri now has a less robotic sound. The new voices are taken from actual individuals to capture more human-like inflection, emphasis, and emotion. Users can choose a voice based on what appeals to them the most.

Individual voice commands

Users can create unique voice shortcuts to have Siri perform numerous activities with a single phrase and quicker response times to existing commands. This enables the automation of routine operations or procedures tailored to the user's needs.

Additional Home Control Capabilities

To operate more devices and appliances in a user's smart home ecosystem, Siri expands the HomeKit integration. By simply asking Siri, complex automation routines can be set up and turned on. Additionally, more vendors are integrating Siri compatibility.

A better CarPlay experience

Along with the performance improvements, Siri's interface on CarPlay is improved for in-car use. The assistant can add more logical turn-by-turn directions and recommend exciting places to stop along the way. Siri on CarPlay is also offline-compatible.

Overall, Siri's numerous upgrades in iOS 17 enable Apple to realize its ambition of a knowledgeable voice assistant. While upholding strict data privacy, the enhancements improve the assistant's comprehension, knowledge, response, and contextual awareness. An exceptionally helpful and knowledgeable digital assistant is available for iOS users.

Press and hold the Home button to request Siri's assistance or say "Hey Siri."

CHAPTER 9

NEW KEYBOARD FEATURES

With iOS 17, the iPhone and iPad's standard on-screen keyboard and typing experience have significantly improved. Apple has incorporated new capabilities and made optimizations to improve typing speed, accuracy, and customization to each user's individual typing style.

Automated Dictation

With iOS 17, text-to-speech dictation is substantially more intelligent. The dictation tool can automatically punctuate your spoken words by adding commas, periods, question marks, and exclamation points as necessary. Based on context, the dictation algorithm also recognizes when you want to add things like newlines or emoji and automatically adds them.

Voice-to-Text Transcribing More Rapidly

Along with improved dictation, iOS 17 also has a quicker transcription process. The voice recognition engine uses cutting-edge machine learning to reduce latency and increase accuracy. So that you can write up your thoughts more quickly, dictated sections are transcribed up to twice as quickly.

Individualised Cursor Control

The text cursor movement settings in iOS 17 can be customized when text is edited. Swiping across the keyboard, pushing the spacebar firmly to activate cursor mode, or tapping the text bar are all options available to users. This enables individual preference-based cursor control selection.

One-handed Typing

With the touch of a button, the system keyboard moves left or right for more straightforward one-handed typing. You can now type words more comfortably without constantly using both hands.

Expanded selection of emoji

The iOS keyboard now has more than 50 new emoji that fall into new categories, including hand movements, everyday objects, gender-inclusive alternatives, and more. An emoji search option makes the ideal emoji from the enormous assortment much faster. Emojis that are frequently used are also put to a favorites list.

Individual Text Replacement

iOS 17 enables the creation of user-defined custom text replacement shortcuts that function similarly to autocorrect. You could configure "omw" to expand to "On my way!" and "em" to include your email address, for instance. The time-saving shortcuts are tailored to your typing style.

Smart Text Selection

Smart text selection simplifies choosing a text for copying, cutting, or pasting. iOS 17 automatically detects whole word or sentence borders when you tap and drag to highlight text, even if you don't drag precisely across them. This increases the efficiency and speed of text manipulation.

Split-tap Typing

Similar to Android's swipe typing, split-tap typing lets users enter words by just tapping the left or right side of the keyboard in iOS 17. Instead of typing out entire words, each letter is intelligently deduced based on chance and context.

Bilingual support

The iOS keyboard now allows simultaneous use of two languages. When you switch languages, the keyboard automatically identifies it and adjusts its word predictions. This makes it possible to communicate in two languages fluently without physically switching keyboards.

Extensions for other keyboards

With iOS 17, third-party keyboards like SwiftKey and Google Keyboard can now be more fully integrated and customized. Custom keyboard developers can provide enhancement features like cursor control, split-tap typing, emoji search, and more.

Sophisticated prediction engine

The word prediction algorithm has been improved to more accurately consider your typing style and vocabulary while reducing errors. It considers various elements and settings, including messaging design, language, and frequently used emoji. Even whole sentences can be predicted by the system with remarkable precision.

Customizable Haptic Keypress Feedback

The haptic feedback intensity on each key press can be fine-tuned in iOS. You can change the feedback's intensity or turn it off entirely. New long-press feedback vibrations and delete key intensity settings are also available. Search for haptics that meet your preferences.

Adaptive Colours for Themes

Depending on the open app, the system keyboard alternates between light and dark themes. Based on whether an app has a light or dark interface, the choice of keyboard color is intelligently synchronized. This makes everything more visible and creates a more seamless experience.

Editing Rich Text

With iOS 17, you can use the keyboard to add rich text styles like bold, italics, underlining, striking through, and font color while editing text. Choose the style from the contextual toolbar directly above the keyboard after selecting the text—no need to go to a different menu.

Grammar Checking Software

With an integrated grammar checker, iOS 17 elevates autocorrect to a new level. It may reorganize entire phrases to suit proper grammatical structure and correct spelling errors. Just one more method iOS aids in the creation of error-free writing.

With all these new and enhanced typing functions, the iOS keyboard is more streamlined, natural, and user-friendly than ever. The improvements in iOS 17 truly optimize the user experience for any requirement, whether you want to type exceptionally quickly for chatting or produce lengthy articles. Apple has raised the bar for mobile text entry and editing.

CHAPTER 10

PHOTOS IMPROVEMENTS

With the release of iOS 17, the Photos app for iPhone and iPad will receive an upgrade with practical new capabilities to improve managing, editing, and sharing photos. Please continue reading for a list of the best photography features added to iOS 17 and detailed instructions on utilizing them.

Additional Photo Editing Tools

You can now fine-tune photographs directly on your device with the sophisticated new adjustment features of the built-in Photos editor. The new editing choices and instructions are as follows:

► Brighten or darken specific areas of a photo using **selective exposure**. Move the slider left or right over the desired area to change exposure. This feature is fantastic for repairing under- or overexposed photos.

► With just one swipe, **Colour Harmony** applies a harmonious color palette from your image to provide an eye-catching, coordinated aesthetic.

► **Modern Matte** increases softness and desaturates colors to provide a crisp, matte appearance and reduces glare that can be distracting.

- **Vibrance** enhances or reduces the intensity of color for strong or subtle impact.

- A **vignette** is a creative technique that uses darkened, blurred corners and edges to attract attention to the center of the image.

- **Sharpen/Soften:** One can add crisp sharpness or diffuse softness by lightly brushing over select regions. This eliminates haziness.

- **Noise Reduction** eliminates grainy noise in low-light images through noise reduction. Select automatic noise reduction or manually modify the strength.

How to Edit in Photos:

- In the Photos app, select a photo, then hit Edit.

- To enlarge the editing toolbar, tap the three dots.

- Pick a tool or filter to use. Change the settings as necessary.

- To make changes and to undo edits, tap Done or Revert.

Sorting Memories

Images are now categorized using cutting-edge AI in the Photos' Memories tab into several relevant occasions and thematic categories. This makes it simpler to find fantastic images again.

Themed Memories: Photos collected by theme, such as landscapes, buildings, animals, weddings, birthdays, etc., makeup themed memories.

Event Memories: Pictures arranged according to specific journeys, holidays, and dates to recall moments.

Alignment Directions

New alignment guidelines have been added to editing tools like Crop to aid in getting exact symmetry or positioning while moving or modifying photos.

Open the crop interface for the desired image and move the corners. Green alignment lines will appear to aid in leveling, orienting, or centering the crop area.

Muted Videos Clips

Now, the Photos app has a simple method for muting video audio.

How to silence a video

► In Photos, choose the video, then select Edit.

► At the top, click the Volume icon.

► Reduce the volume to mute by dragging it down.

► This is excellent for taking out distracting background noise from clips.

Video in Portrait Mode

With the release of iOS 17, the video now has a Portrait option for creative background blurring. Similar to how images taken in Portrait mode operate.

To apply it:

► Swipe left to enter video mode after opening the Camera.

► Select Portrait (the face icon) from the top menu.

► Put your subject in the center of the frame. The

background will get blurry.

▶ Press Record to begin filming in portrait mode!

Live Text with Images

The Live Text feature now functions straight in Photos. You can copy or share text that has been selected in an image.

Text extraction:

▶ Open a picture with legible text.

▶ Tap and hold the text, and a menu will appear.

▶ To remove text from an image, select Copy Text or Share Text.

Visual Lookup

You can use Visual Look Up to learn more about things, places, and scenes identified in pictures. This helps you discover more about the subjects or locations of your photos. To get more context and details about an image, swipe up on it in Photos.

To give it a try:

▶ Swipe up from the bottom of an image that is open in Photos.

- ► Information cards will appear in Visual Look Up if an object or location is recognized.

- ► For further information, click links to view Wikipedia or other web pages.

iCloud Shared Library

Five additional individuals can now share photos in your iCloud Photos collection. Take advantage of a seamless shared album update as you all upload pictures.

To share a library:

- ► To access the photos, go to Settings > [your name] > iCloud > Photos.

- ► Tap Share My Library

- ► To share with, enter names or Apple IDs. Then, set the permissions.

- ► App alerts inviting users to the shared library will be sent to invited users.

CHAPTER 11

NEW MAPS CAPABILITIES

New capabilities have been added to iOS 17's Maps, including viewing real-time traffic conditions and obtaining instructions for electric vehicles.

Virtual City Experience in 3D

A remarkably detailed 3D map view that brings the cityscape to life is now available for some major cities. Explore and navigate using detailed 3D building models, raised terrain, trees, and other features.

To make the 3D Map active:

▶ Look for a supported city, such as San Francisco or London.

- ➤ Tap the 3D button at the bottom and pinch out to zoom in on a specific location.
- ➤ The new 3D map mode will come into view.
- ➤ You may rotate, pan, and zoom to see the city in 3D.

Real-Time Transit Improvements

In iOS 17, maps and directions for public Transit are more thorough and precise. Buses, trains, ferries, and other vehicles are all displayed with accurate locations in real-time.

Real-Time Transit usage:

► Put your location in Maps.

► Tap Transit to display available means of transport.

► The Map displays local stations as well as train and bus arrival schedules.

► To see movement in real-time on the Map, tap a route.

Comprehensive Airport Maps

The coverage and level of detail on airport terminal and gate maps have been significantly increased. Visualize check-in areas, security, gates, services, etc. in 3D.

To see a map of the airport

- ▶ Look up the name or code of an airport.
- ▶ Select the airport or terminal name.
- ▶ Choose View 3D Map from the menu.
- ▶ To explore various locations, use Zoom and rotation.

Locations to Charge Evs

Locating somewhere to charge your electric car while you're on the go is simple with Maps. Nearby charging stations are automatically surfaced.

To discover local EV chargers:

- ▶ In the top-right corner, tap the layers button.
- ▶ Activate Electric Vehicle Charging under Services.
- ▶ On the Map, nearby chargers will be highlighted.
- ▶ To view charger types, availability, etc., tap one.

Enhanced offline maps

Offline maps now have more information, such as heights, landmarks, building models, parking lots, and exits.

To pre-download an offline map:

- ► Look up the location on the Maps screen.
- ► Select Download Map by tapping the three dots in the corner.
- ► Choose the region's size before saving it offline.
- ► To download the area to your device, tap Download.

Accurate Building footprints

Maps, even those of rural and distant locations, provide more precise information about the shapes and sizes of buildings. This is useful for improved distances and orientation.

To view better architectural forms:

- ► Zoom in on a region filled with buildings.
- ► The Map will display the boundaries and footprints of the buildings.

➤ To compare satellite and conventional views, switch between map modes.

Redesigned place cards

A totally revamped place card with essential details like hours, photographs, ratings, reviews, and more can be displayed by tapping a location.

To view the new place cards:

➤ On the Map, perform a search or press any location.

➤ The updated cards have a straightforward layout.

➤ The card's expanded details can be seen by scrolling down.

➤ To find out more, click links to the website, menu, or reviews.

CHAPTER 12

ENHANCED SECURITY FEATURES

With each new iOS iteration, Apple has constantly prioritized increasing security. The release of iOS 17 includes significant improvements to safeguard user data and stop unauthorized access. This section will highlight the significant security improvements users can use after updating to the most recent OS version.

End-to-end encryption

The introduction of end-to-end encryption for Apple's native apps is one of iOS 17's most significant security upgrades. So that only the sender and receiver can access message contents, communication through services like FaceTime and Messages will be secured. Even Apple cannot see them. This stops outsiders from listening in on users' private talks.

Two-factor authentication and stronger passwords

Password improvements introduced in iOS 17 will assist users in creating stronger passwords for their accounts. The software will alert users when they use weak passwords that are simple to guess and urge them to strengthen them by including extra letters, digits, and symbols.

Two-factor authentication will be prompted more frequently to provide protection beyond passwords. Account protection will be increased by including features like Face ID, security keys, and verification codes.

Enhancements to iCloud Keychain and Autofill

The security features of iCloud Keychain, which houses credit card information and passwords, will be improved. Users of iOS 17 can expressly enable two-factor authentication and more excellent encryption for the iCloud Keychain.

Only credentials from apps that the user has already given permission to use will be suggested and filled up by Autofill with iCloud Keychain. This stops unauthorized programs from stealthily obtaining information or saving passwords.

Continual Security Updates

iOS 17 allows automated background installation of security updates, ensuring users receive timely security fixes. This indicates that they will be implemented as soon as critical updates to remedy vulnerabilities are released. Users are no longer required to initiate updates manually.

VPN Service built-in

Apple's iVPN, an integrated virtual private network (VPN) service with specialized encryption, is available with iOS 17. By routing traffic over an encrypted tunnel, iVPN secures all network conversations and online activity. This stops hacking into public Wi-Fi networks.

Additional Private Access Tokens

To improve protection against unauthorized logins, Private Access Tokens for Sign In with Apple have been updated. To produce and store tokens more securely, iOS 17 uses cutting-edge cryptographic methods. Unknown devices' sign-in attempts will result in further identification verification.

More effective data separation between apps

More robust separation between app and OS functions is now possible thanks to updates to the iOS architecture. Each app can only access specific user data and device components based on permissions. Overall, privacy is improved, and vulnerabilities are decreased.

A better anti-phishing/malware detection system

For more effective malware and complex phishing attack detection and blocking, new machine-learning capabilities have been added to iOS 17—automatic detection and blocking of phishing links that pose as authentic websites. The downloaded files will undergo a malware signature scan.

Integrated App Behaviour Monitoring

Users of iOS 17 have access to detailed reports showing how each program uses the Camera, microphone, and other sensor hardware. This is so that rights can be withdrawn when any odd or unnecessary app behavior is detected. Thus, covert exploitation of sensitive user data is avoided.

Access Restricted by Time to Sensitive Assets

Now, strictly regulated temporary access will be provided to apps requesting one-time access to private user information like location or contacts. Developers must indicate the timescale required; after that period ends, access is automatically withdrawn.

Regarding user privacy and security, iOS 17 significantly improved thanks to several changes to the operating system, apps, and services. Apple is still at the forefront of safeguarding iPad and iPhone customers from new online threats. All iOS users should prioritize implementing these newest security features.

CHAPTER 13

SPLIT SCREEN

The split-screen multitasking capability on the iPhone enables you to run two apps simultaneously. This can be useful for several things, such as checking email while looking over the web or watching a video and taking notes.

How to use split-screen

These procedures should be followed to use the split screen on iOS 17:

► The first app you want to utilize in split-screen should be opened.

► Swipe up from the bottom of the screen after starting the app to reveal the Dock.

► Touch and hold the second app you wish to utilize in the split screen once you've located it.

► Drag the app icon from the Dock to the left or right border of the screen.

► The second application will show up in split-screen mode.

► You can change their sizes by sliding the line between the two apps. Swipe up on an app's icon to close it from the split screen.

Which iOS 17 apps
enable split-screen?

On iOS 17, not all applications allow split-screen. Many well-known apps, like Safari, Mail, Messages, Notes, and Maps, do, though. The App Store has a list of all the apps that support split-screen.

Some pointers for iOS 17's split-screen mode

Following are some pointers for utilizing split screen on iOS 17:

- ► Swipe left or right on the dividing line to swiftly switch between apps when they are split-screen.

- ► Drag the icon of a third app from the Dock to the top of the screen to launch it in split-screen mode.

- ► Open the app twice if you want to use a split screen with two instances of the same program.

- ► Drag the dividing line to the screen's edge to lock the size of an app in a split screen.

- ► On iOS 17, is it possible to force a split screen?

- ► On iOS 17, there is currently no option to force a split screen. A few third-party apps, though, can assist you in doing this. Split Screen Enabler is one such app.

CHAPTER 14

USING YOUR DEVICE WITH THE NEW IOS 17

How to Use the Home Screen

Your Apple device's Home Screen serves as its primary display. You may access your widgets, apps, and other features there.

You can perform the following to personalize the Home Screen:

► **Add or Remove Apps:** Tap and hold an app until it jiggles to add or uninstall it. Drag the app to the desired location after that. Also, you can drag an application to the screen's bottom to remove it.

► **Making folders:** Tap and hold an app until it jiggles. After that, drag another app over it. A folder will be automatically created.

► **Replace the wallpaper:** Select a new wallpaper by going to Settings > Wallpaper.

► **Add widgets:** Tap and hold a blank area of the Home Screen to add a widget. Next, select Widgets. Drag the widget you want to add to the desired spot after choosing it.

How to Use the Lock Screen

The screen that appears when you power on or wake up your iPhone is known as the Lock Screen. You can check the time, date, notifications, and other data.

You can perform the following to personalize the Lock Screen:

► **Change the widgets:** Tap and hold an open area on the Lock Screen. Next, select Widgets. Drag the widget you want to add to the desired spot after choosing it.

► **Personalize:** Select Personalize from Settings > Lock screen. Here, you can customize the look of your Lock Screen and the apps and notifications that appear on it.

Using Messages

You send and receive text messages, images, videos, and other types of content using the Messages app.

Open the Messages app and tap on the person you wish to communicate with to send a message. Type your message and press Send after that.

Tapping the Attachment icon, you can transmit additional stuff, such as pictures, videos, and documents.

Open the Messages app and hit the Plus icon to start a group chat. Next, pick the individuals you wish to include in the group chat.

Open the Messages app and hit the App Store button to use iMessage apps. Choose the iMessage apps that you want to use next.

Using FaceTime

You can use FaceTime to video call other iPhone, iPad, or Mac users.

Open the FaceTime app, then tap on the person you wish to call to start a FaceTime call. Tap the Video button after that. You can also place a Face-

Time call from the Control Center or the Lock Screen.

Open the FaceTime application and place a call to use SharePlay. Then, select the content you wish to share by tapping the SharePlay button.

Using Photos

You can store, manage, and edit your photographs and videos with photos.

Open the Photos app, then tap the desired album or photo to begin using Photos. Then, you can do any of the following:

▶ Tap an image or video to view it.

▶ Tap the Edit button to make changes to a photo or video.

▶ Tap the Share button to share a picture or a video.

▶ Make a fresh album: Click the plus button, then choose New Album.

▶ Sort out your images and videos: Drag and drop the images and videos into the desired albums after tapping the Albums tab.

Using Music

The music-listening app you use is called Music. Launch the Music app and tap the desired album, song, or playlist to utilize Music. Then, you can take any of the following actions:

- ➤ Tap to start a song.
- ➤ Tap the Pause button to pause the song.
- ➤ Tap Next to go to the Next song
- ➤ Return to the prior song by selecting "Previous."
- ➤ Turn up the volume: Slide the volume knob.
- ➤ Make a fresh playlist: Click the plus button, then choose New Playlist.
- ➤ Including songs in the playlists: After tapping the playlist, press the plus button. Choose the Music you want to include.

CHAPTER 15

USING SAFARI

In iOS 17, the Safari web browser receives exciting new features to improve browsing convenience, performance, and privacy.

Quicker page load

Safari now uses background pre-fetching of linked pages to significantly speed up page loading times after you tap a link. Instant page loading occurs.

To facilitate quicker page loads:

▶ Select Settings > Safari.

▶ Turn "Faster Page Loads" on in the General section.

► If you hover over links, pre-fetched pages will now load

More effective intelligent tracking prevention

In iOS 17, the Intelligent Tracking Prevention function, which prevents cross-site trackers, becomes even more intelligent to recognize and thwart more advanced advertising tactics. Your online activities are kept more secret.

Push Notifications on the Web

Even if the website isn't open in a tab, Safari can now permit websites to deliver notifications. Allow push notifications for your favourite websites' updates.

To make web notifications available:

► Any website's "aA" button should be tapped, and then "Allow Notifications" should be chosen.

► You will be asked by Safari to confirm allowing alerts. Click Allow.

> Now, even when the website is closed, alerts can be sent.

Shared Tab Groups

Tab groups let you save and distribute collections of websites for others to view or access. Excellent for shopping, organizing trips, and other activities.

Making a tab group

> Open several tabs dedicated to a project or topic.

> For a group to start, drag one tab onto another. Name the group.

> To create a link to share the group, tap "Share Tabs."

Enhancing Tab Management

Additionally, you can hide tabs, pin your favorite tabs so they always stay at the top, and create colorful tab folders to organize your open tabs further.

To control tabs:

> To see administration options, tap and hold a tab.

➤ To group tabs into a folder, drag them together.

➤ To temporarily hide a tab, tap "Hide Tab."

➤ To keep it always at the top and visible, tap "Pin Tab."

Grid View in Desktop Class Tabs

All of your open tabs are now shown in a grid in Safari, so you can quickly browse through them. To switch to grid mode, click the tab view's up arrow.

Using Tab Grid:

➤ On the open tabs view, scroll up.

➤ The layout will enlarge into a grid with tab previews.

➤ To open a tab, tap any thumbnail.

Integration of Passkey

Safari supports passkeys for password-free website sign-ins. Passkeys, generated on the device, provide biometric security for account access.

Using Passkeys

➤ Select the Sign in with Passkey option on the login screen for the website.

➤ To authenticate with Face ID or Touch ID, follow the steps.

➤ You can now securely access a website account!

Internet Translation

With just one swipe, Safari can now instantly translate an entire webpage between more than 100 languages. Web browser extensions are not required.

Page translation

➤ Translate a Page by tapping the "Aa" button.

➤ From the pop-up list, select the source and target languages.

➤ Web page text will be automatically translated.

Stocks and Weather Widgets

New Weather and Stocks widgets have been added to Safari's tools panel to access essential data while browsing quickly. Your favorite cities and stocks can be customized.

To add widgets:

➤ Select Tools by tapping the compass icon.

➤ Scroll through the toolbar and select Customise.

➤ Add widgets for the weather and stocks to the panel.

➤ Setup location and investment preference

CHAPTER 16

TIPS AND TRICKS FOR USING iOS 17

9 Tips for Getting Used to the New Look and Feel of iOS 17

1. To eliminate distractions like distracting Home screen widgets, use focus modes.
2. Sort and filter apps in the App Library to organize them in a different order.
3. Try out new widget designs and wallpapers.
4. Add or remove controls to personalize the Control Centre.
5. For greater immersion, turn on haptics and spatial audio.
6. Try out the Messages' Memoji modifications.
7. In Accessibility, change the font size, color

scheme, and contrast.

8. Turn on the updated clock and weather icon styles.

9. Try dark mode for a brand-new look to discover hidden gesture adjustments like swipe typing.

12 Strategies to Improve iOS 17's Battery Life

1. Limit background app refresh and activate Low Power Mode

2. For programs that don't require them, turn off location services

3. Reduce screen brightness and the duration of auto-lock

4. Reduce motion effects and turn off live wallpapers

5. Halt automated app updates and downloads

6. For apps you almost ever use, turn off background app refresh.

7. Disable Hey Siri if you don't use it.

8. Reduce battery aging by using optimized charging.

9. Verify the battery's health to determine its

capacity.

10.Change the watch face or turn off Bluetooth when not necessary.

11.OLED panels' Dark Mode can be turned on to save energy.

12.Reduce cellular power consumption by using Low Data Mode.

6 Tips for Using Picture-in-Picture Mode on iOS 17

1. Swiping up from the bottom corner of a video will launch PiP.

2. Position the PiP window on the screen by dragging it.

3. To change the PiP floating window's size, pinch.

4. To end PiP and return to the fullscreen video, swipe up.

5. Start PiP first to keep it playing after locking your iPhone.

6. Double-tap the PiP window to go into or out of fullscreen.

10 Tips for Using the App Library to Organise Your Apps

1. Use the Search tab to find any app quickly.

2. In the App Library, switch on alphabetical sorting.

3. Make your own Smart Folders for categories like "Games" and "Social," for example.

4. Remove unwanted apps from the App Library.

5. To solely utilize the App Library view, turn off app pages.

6. Move apps that have lately been added to a readily accessible folder

7. To rapidly edit, share, or remove an app icon from the App Library view, tap and hold it.

8. Remove App Recommendations by turning off Show Suggestions

9. Use the Other Apps folder in the App Library for less often used apps.

10. Swipe down on the status bar from anywhere to access the App Library immediately.

8 Tips for Mastering Using Widgets on the Home Screen

1. Widgets can be resized by pinching to enlarge them.

2. Drag widgets on top of one another to stack them all in one location.

3. You can view, manage, and edit your widgets by tapping and holding the Home Screen.

4. You can find third-party widgets by touching and holding the Home Screen and tapping the + icon.

5. You can get widget suggestions by pressing and holding an empty space on the Home Screen.

6. Widgets can be moved anywhere on the Home Screen, including between apps.

7. Tap and hold a widget that is compatible with the app to see more interactive information and controls.

8. To update a widget or access actions and information that pertain to it, touch and hold it.

7 Guidelines for Simplifying Notification Handling

1. Combine notifications that aren't time-sensitive into a daily summary

2. When focused, use focus modes to turn off certain apps' notifications.

3. Designate VIP contacts who always call or message you.

4. Put unknown callers on silence to lessen interruptions from spam calls.

5. Long-press an app icon, then select Notifications to manage notifications.

6. By dismissing the summary alert, you can quickly clear a notification alert.

7. Swipe actions for each app can be customized in Settings > Notifications > (app name)

10 Tips for Using the New Multitasking Features in iOS 17

1. In an app, long-press the Stage Manager icon to access Split View.

2. Drag the dividing line to resize the columns in the Split View.

3. Drag the dividing line to the screen's edge to end Split View.

4. You can open multiple apps simultaneously by clicking and holding an app's icon in the App Library and dragging it.

5. Swipe up from the bottom of the screen, pause on an app, and then swipe further to use Slide Over.

6. You can switch between Slide Over apps by quickly swiping left/right at the bottom of the display.

7. You can view all of its open windows by touching an app's icon in the App Switcher.

8. Swipe a window off the top of the screen to close it in multitasking view.

9. When in Split View, double-tap the app's divider to go to full screen.

10. When using supported apps, enable multiple windows by touching their icon in the App Switcher.

8 Tips for Using the iOS 17 Camera to Take Better Pictures

1. Before taking a picture, press and hold the shutter button to lock the focus.
2. Tap the face or other region of the subject to change exposure.
3. While holding down the shutter button, take pictures in QuickTake mode.
4. Bring the Camera up close to the subject to turn on Macro mode for close-up photographs.
5. You can see what's outside the frame by tapping the viewfinder's edges.
6. Utilise Night mode to overcome difficult lighting conditions.
7. Using Portrait Lighting makes portraits look more professional.
8. You can access pro-level options like ISO, shutter speed, and white balance by swiping up.

6 Suggestions for Maximizing Share Play Sessions

1. By touching the SharePlay symbol during a FaceTime session, you can launch SharePlay.
2. Together with friends, browse and simultaneously play Music or TV episodes.
3. Utilize the shared progress bar to sync your exercise progress.
4. To view apps and browse the web together, share your screen.
5. Sharing controller capabilities while playing together
6. To multitask while still enjoying SharePlay media, use Picture-in-Picture.

12 Tips for iOS 17 Safari Upgrades for Safer Browsing

1. Activate Safari's built-in monitoring feature for passwords used in security breaches.
2. Allow websites to send you alerts by using the new web push notifications.
3. Websites can be automatically translated into the language of your choice.

4. Create separate tab groups for each browsing session to facilitate cleanup.

5. Saved passwords can be summarised for convenience and security.

6. To approve payments on websites without providing credit card information, use Apple Pay.

7. Automatically fill in verification codes that reputable websites send to your phone.

8. Change the privacy settings in Safari to enable the Private Relay encryption protection.

9. Use the Intelligent Tracking Prevention feature in Safari to stop cross-site tracking.

10. Always-opening tabs in Private mode for discreet browsing

11. Enable the password monitoring function in Safari to look for compromised credentials.

12. On your iPhone, activate Siri to start a web search from your current location swiftly.

CHAPTER 17

LOOKING AHEAD TO FUTURE iOS UPDATES

Even though iOS 17 has many new features, iOS development is ongoing. Apple is already working diligently on iOS 18 and afterward. Here are some reasonable estimates for what potential future iOS releases might include:

1. Updates to the new interface that will be unveiled with iOS 17. Apple changes the UI every year, adding new widgets, icons, default apps, and more. We'll have to wait and see what iOS 18's design modifications will be.

2. Support for Matter expansion. The foundation for Matter, the new smart home connectivity standard, is laid by iOS 17. Expect upcoming

iOS to include deeper integration and automation tools once Matter devices are available.

3. New workflows and shortcuts in the Shortcuts app. The Shortcuts app is still a go-to for power users. Advanced users expect more triggers and scripting possibilities to increase the system's capabilities.

4. Potential growth of new iOS 17 features like Live Activities, MultiTouch for iPadOS, and Share-Play. Throughout several iOS versions, Apple frequently builds on significant new features.

5. Greater adoption of Passkeys for logins without a password. Passkeys have yet to be widely used, but iOS 17 lays the stage. With other iOS, this might change.

6. A further advance in AI's capacity for processing natural language. Apple takes pleasure in being a machine learning pioneer; thus, advancements in AI will continue.

7. New accessibility features expanding on Live Captions in iOS 17's updates. Apple still places a lot of emphasis on inclusivity.

8. More options for adjusting iOS' appearance and

feel to user liking. The new theming choices in iOS 17 might become more extensive.

9. Battery performance and life will continue to increase, perhaps with quicker adoption of new silicon. The A17 chip will probably follow.

CONCLUSION

I recommend updating to iOS 17 if you own an iPhone. It is a significant update that adds many new features and enhancements that will increase your iPhone's functionality, adaptability, and user-friendliness.